Death in Summer
Maung Day

DEATH IN SUMMER

ဝေရာသီတွင် သေဆုံးခြင်း

MAUNG DAY

CHIN MUSIC
P R E S S

BOOK AND COVER DESIGN BY Marc Katz

ISBN 9781634050500

LIBRARY OF CONGRESS CONTROL NUMBER 2023933229

PRINTED IN Canada

PUBLISHED BY Chin Music Press

1501 Pike Place #329
Seattle, Washington 98101
www.chinmusicpress.com

Chin Music Press is based in the traditional territory of the Coast
Salish People, the Duwamish (dxʷdəwʔabš), in land that touches
the shared ancestral waters of the Suquamish (dxʷsəq̓ʷəb), Tulalip
(dxʷliləp), and Muckleshoot (bəqəlšuɫ) Nations. We honor the
people past, present, and future who belong to this place.

CHIN MUSIC
P R E S S

For my grandmother, Khin Nu,
and my friend, the great late Burmese poet Lu Sann.

Table of Contents

II

Introduction

"Mirages Move Quietly":
Revolt and Rest in Maung Day's *Death in Summer*

I

I first met Maung Day and encountered his writing in September 2017, when he was visiting Seattle for a few days as part of the University of Iowa's International Writing Program. It was late summer, and the city was still in its relaxed seasonal state. I picked up the writer on a random street corner downtown, near the waterfront. His dark hair flashing across his face. He was composed, present, eager, and tired. He chose to visit Seattle because he grew up with grunge music and had heard about Seattle's literary community. The poet Rauan Klassnik had made the initial connection, and so it was I who would introduce Maung Day to the Emerald City. Across several hours I showed him around the weave of the city's blocks and neighborhoods. We discussed local poetry scenes, Seattle's music culture and its famous musicians, the political cacophony across the United States, and, of course, events in Myanmar. Each instant was fueled with questions, conversations, and image-making, and when our time together was up, I watched Maung Day return to his hotel, his silhouette slowly fading back into the stricter schedule and program.

In March 2019, I went to visit Maung Day and his community of poets and artists in Yangon. Myanmar was going through yet another chapter of political tension and social conflict with Rohingya persecuted and Aung San Suu Kyi once again in the spotlight with complicity. Another spin of the wheel, another teetering on the edge of stability, a general sense of unease, and also an opening up: Myanmar was actively making it, for the first time in years, easier for foreign tourists to visit and experience the country. I met Maung Day with a poetic urgency, a drive to sneak through the door while it was still propped open, and our time together was exuberant.

We explored much of Maung Day's homeland, our minds bouncing along with the bumps of the bus and motorbike, through spins of dust on road and trail. I met numerous poet friends, attended readings, and stumbled into gallery exhibitions. I learned a crucial fact: poetry is intensely interconnected with sociopolitical action across the country, and at the center of the action are the poets. In Myanmar the poets are on the front lines of any demonstrations, they are at the center of the protests, and they are behind the scenes fueling logistics and communications, offering scathing criticisms of abuse and authoritarianism.

Learning of the role of poetry and poets left me feeling inspired, wanting to stay in touch with Maung Day, wanting to collaborate and share more conversations. Shortly after the visit, we cowrote the bilingual poetry collection *Like salt. Like a spine.*, reflective of our shared energies and commitment to a surreal form of witness and projective verse. We found inspiration in our energy, in our spontaneity. The prose poetry arose around us like a cloak. We started the project with writing completely in English, but we decided on a bilingual edition to emphasize our global connection. Maung Day graciously translated the book into Burmese, a limited number of print copies were created in Seattle, and the book was shared to the world as an e-book.

Two years later, in early 2021, Myanmar exploded into another chapter of authoritarianism and protest: the Spring

Revolution, a revolution of the people, a revolution of the poets, following Min Aung Hlaing's February 2021 coup. The world was given a brief glimpse of the demonstrations against the Tatmadaw, mostly on Twitter: scenes of bloody and terrible events rising out of the smoke, and scenes of courage and strength of the people of Myanmar. I watched helplessly from my perch in Seattle, fearing for Maung Day and the community of poet protesters undoubtedly finding their way, their role, their response to systemic inequities and oppressions. When I sent Maung Day an email and didn't get the immediate response, my heart was heavy and dread was thorough.

But then he responded, and we exchanged several emails that amazingly crossed some of that chapter's most violent moments. Maung Day used temporary email accounts and maintained a low profile, but continued his spirit of goodwill and confidence: bravery in the face of antagonism, disintegration of community, violence of the oppressor, tribulations and trauma throughout his homeland. His words and actions were endearing, confident, filled with purpose. He shared his work, his passion, and his relentless commitment to writing and visual art. Meanwhile, the country continued to erupt into action, and Burmese poets from all over continued to protest. Many sang their songs day after day, sometimes at the cost of their lives, the images of their dead bodies appearing on social media. The threads of poets' dialogue passing along the digital vacuum like whispers in the dark.

II

Today the world grinds forward. The Burmese military continues to hold the country by its throat and like many on the outside, I know little. Myanmar, like so much of the world, is smothered with blankets of authoritarian rule, where social media is limited, and any formal journalism only shows up in scattered bits and pieces. But like a beacon, Maung Day's *Death in Summer* has appeared. It feels more important than a news headline, social media thread, or email: the release is monumental, collecting the mind and memories of a poet whose poetry is an everyday reflection of life under the pound of the regime.

Each piece in *Death in Summer* feels raw, exposing hardship and brutality alongside hope and the future-thinking of the poet across multiple chapters and settings. Maung Day's works reflect urban and rural life in an array of contexts, capturing the unique space between the private and the public, the individual and the elective. "The city is trembling with insomnia," he writes in "Night in the City." In "Tongueless Children," Maung Day comments on the ironies and contradictions of social circumstance: "There is a school for the children with no tongues who were born to tongueless mothers. The school teaches only one subject: patience."

Maung Day's new collection is the latest in a long tradition of Burmese poets releasing works that comment on everyday life in Myanmar, a country plagued with military coups, immense poverty, and violent suppression of thoughts and ideas. It follows traditions of humor and absurdity, while maintaining a subtext of necessary outcry towards injustice, and a yearning for more: more knowledge, more understanding, and more action. But unlike many of his contemporaries, Maung Day's approach is one of abstraction, centering the grotesque, and finding significance in the fantastical, dreamlike landscapes that may not replace the horror but handle it more openly. His descriptions are often brief, combining concise images with vague settings and contexts. His works uplift and question, and they often seek to disrupt through liberating the imagination.

This book marks Maung Day's first major release in the United States. *Death in Summer* is a fantastic achievement for a poet whose current chapter involves so much brutality and so much loss, through everyday oppression and countless moments of seclusion and isolation for safety. *Death in Summer* is a collection full of surprises and emergence. It is a book of reality and a book of breaking open reality. It is a book that explores the mirages of our daily existence, our shared histories, and our ability to thrive through storytelling and symbol making. The mirages show deferred hope, misunderstanding, temporary solutions, and questioning of meaning. Across trauma, across faux stability, these images emerge, images of consequence and commitment alongside decay and disintegration, a visual and textual phantasmagoria. Each poem emerges as a relic, an offering, a short tale that opens and closes within moments, and the text is interspersed with fantastical black-and-white illustrations, bizarre and hallucinatory with beastly figures and a lingering sense of violence.

With each passing day, we across the globe may not know much about the current struggle of the people of Myanmar. We may be left wondering, but *Death in Summer* reminds us the poets are there, alive, of and with the people of the country, acting and sharing poems through memory, love, determination, and liberation. The pensive and ponderous pieces of *Death in Summer* are one brief illumination opening a path for us all, present and future generations together. Through them we may learn, grow, and understand. These poems emphasize public voice and collective spirit, through suffering and triumph, and yet at the core is Maung Day: his voice, his experience, his self. There he is, ever exploring, ever curious, ever committed to sharing his own visions, his own subtle gestures and mirages, his own passages as we all move forward.

–Greg Bem

I

Migrants

When my grandparents moved to the city, they walked a dirt road that stretched for over a thousand miles. The road smelled of gunpowder and smoke. When it was time for lunch, they sat down and stared at each other until wildflowers sprang up from their eyes. They ate the flowers and continued their journey. Bandits and militias awaited them on their way; my grandparents had to leave their belongings one piece at a time. By the time they got to the city, there were no clothes left on their bodies.

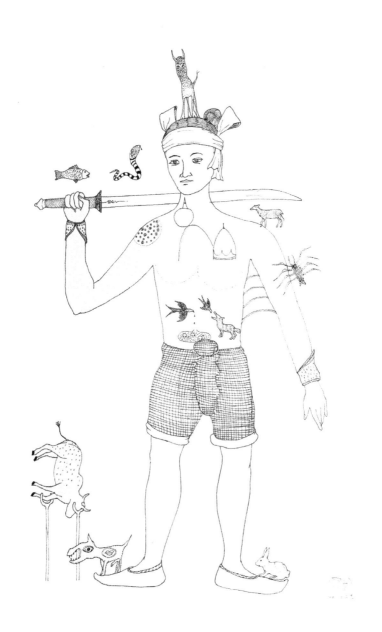

The Heir II, 2018

Fire

My mother is afraid of fire. She has seen villages completely
devoured as if they never existed before. She thinks fire has the
face of a daydreamer. She often says fire is both soft as cotton
and brutal as a tyrant. Every morning, she offers yellow flowers
at the shrine, praying the fire leaves her family alone. There was
this one time when my father told her about a Vietnamese monk.
The monk burned himself to death on the streets of Saigon
protesting against the persecution of the Buddhist monks by the
government. My mother listened to the story and cried, her tears
glistening like salt in the sun.

Thug Nation, 2016

Uncle

After my family moved to the city, one of my uncles visited from a rural town to see us. Upon arriving at our house, he went up the rain tree in our yard instead of coming inside. When I looked up at him, I could only see parts of him between the leaves. My mother needed to shout to have a conversation with him. At night lying in my bed, I heard him singing. His songs were about paddies, rivers, and his dead dog whose ghost came back to see him. My uncle stayed in the tree for a week and went back home.

Yangon, 1988

The tall man in ragged clothes was ordering other men to slit the throat of the policeman. He shouted, "This pig has been sucking our blood for a long time!" Other men did as he said. I was an eight-year-old boy when this happened. But I saw the tall man in ragged clothes again after some years. This time I saw him in a painting in a museum. He was taking a picnic with his family in the shade of a large tree.

Night in the City

Feathers drop from the night sky. The city is trembling with insomnia. The lights go out and street dogs go blind in the dark. I am sitting in my room, listening to the forest in the next room whispering something to the rabbits that burrow under my bed. Children go out on the streets and collect the feathers. On the flip side of the city, birds preen their feathers on the edge of a moon-shaped pool.

A Rainy Day in the City

If you don't look closely, you won't see the city. It sits in a darkness from which it can't rise again. In the drizzling rain, a homeless man stands at the dock beaming like a beacon. Actually, it is no man but a meteor coming down to touch the surface of the river gently. In the drizzling rain, the footbridges of the city burst into flames. A corpse waiting for a burial at a monastery mutters how much he hates the wet days, a corpse that soon will melt into the rain-soaked ground.

.

King of Birds, 2013

Things They Carry

With the night falling, they come into the city. They sleep beside women and they are not the husbands; do surgeries on men and they are not surgeons; bury children in the riverbed and they are not the parents. They dig up earth and demolish old buildings and they are not gravediggers or construction workers. They have flowerpot heads and are not attacked by stray dogs. We follow them and make a list of things they carry. They carry moons, powdered skulls, cans of food, shrapnel wounds of rainbows, bankers, oil tankers. They never leave the city again.

The Guest

When he came into my living room, I was watching TV. He
went straight to the fridge and took the leftovers. He slept on my
couch. The next morning, I had to clean up the couch covered
with scales, his scales, in rainbow colors. The entire place was
riddled with them—the kitchen, the bathroom, the backyard. And
there was no sign of him leaving yet. I told him I didn't know
him and I didn't want him to stay. He said it was totally normal
to walk into any house and stay as a guest. Before he finally left,
he told me to treat the next guest kindly.

Lost Children 3, 2022

Tongueless Children

There is a school for the children with no tongues who were born to tongueless mothers. The school teaches only one subject: patience. "Patience is the greatest virtue in life," say the fathers who can speak. If the children want to express their feelings to their fathers, they must speak through birds given to them on the first day of school. But these birds are not the talking animals like those from children's stories. They relay the feelings of their young masters by making various noises.

One child who starts going to school receives a sparrow from his father. This bird is different from the others. It grows so fast and so large that within a week it becomes the size of a house. The first time it makes noises to relay the boy's feelings to his father, it is so loud the father goes deaf.

Classroom

They came into our classroom. We were just a bunch of kids happy enough to go to school. They put us all together in the middle of the room and summoned rain. Once the rain started, they hurried outside and shut us in. The ceiling turned into a dark sheet of rain clouds, and water poured down. We were left soaking wet in a rain that never stopped.

Cities in His Scabs

A boy with scabs that itch and ache. There are cities in
his scabs—cities filled with people, supermarkets, pets,
automobiles. In one of the cities where there is night in some
parts and morning in others, where summer and winter come
simultaneously, the boy's mother lives. Every day, she goes around
looking for him, shouting his name. But she will never find him.

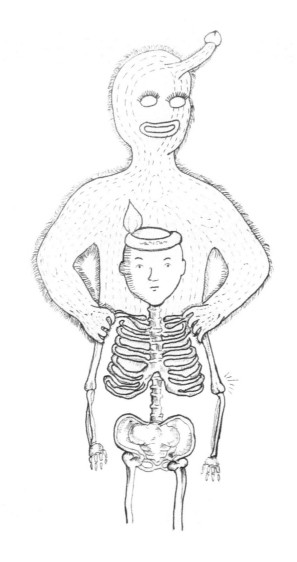

My Duty is to Protect Him #1, 2012

Burning Down the School

A madman builds a town in his head, and a boy goes to school in that town. The boy who has blinking fairy lights for eyes and an exhaust pipe emitting pink smoke for a mouth meets a girl and falls for her instantly. There is a tree in the boy's head, and birds resting on its branches are his dreams. His friends shoot the birds down with slingshots, his parents cut down the tree with a chainsaw, and the girl doesn't love him back. One night the boy sneaks out and burns down the school. The flames snap at the night sky with their exquisite teeth.

Lost Children 5, 2022

A Soldier's Return

After fighting in a war, a soldier comes home on just one leg.
There are riots everywhere in the city. Blood on the streets.
When he gets home, there is no one in the house. His wife has
left him for another man. His parents have died. That night
he takes a bronze bell to a field and rings it repeatedly until a
thousand crows swoop in from all directions and tear up his body.
After the feast of the crows, there's nothing left of him except his
bones and scraps of his uniform.

The Magician

Riots night and day. People desperately need something to enjoy, some sort of entertainment that would make them forget all the horrors taking place in the city. Luckily, a magician comes to them. People build a large stage for him with much excitement. The magician goes up the stage pulling a rope. At the end of the rope, a horse. He then enters the body of the beast through the butthole. People wait to see what would happen next. Absolutely nothing happens. There's just the horse standing on the stage. Then time passes and winter comes.

A Prisoner Writes a Poem

Prison days are long. Boredom eats away at the inmates. Some
pick up hobbies to kill time. One political prisoner decides to
try his hand at writing poetry. He smuggles in some chalk, and
when the night falls, he tries to write a poem on the wall. But he
can't. Writing poetry, he finds, isn't as easy as he thinks. He prays
to the guardian spirit of poetry. Still, no poem comes to him.
But one night as he sits leaning against the wall in desperation,
a woman appears in front of him. While he stares at her in
amazement, the woman transforms into smoke, enters his mouth,
and disappears. That night, he writes a poem.

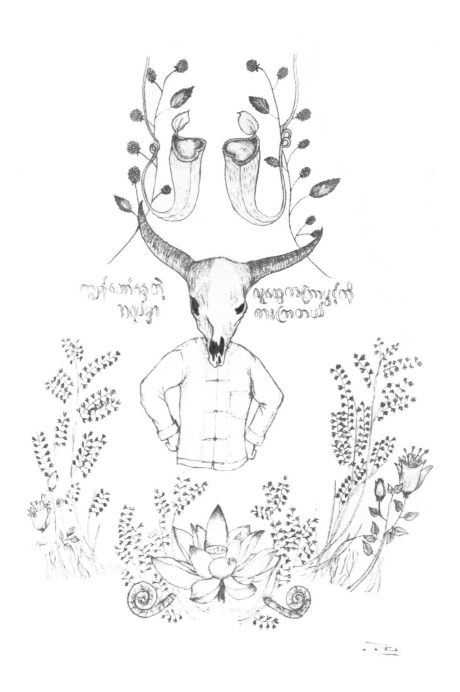

Where I Come From, People Eat Lotuses, 2014

Beneath the Stars

A political prisoner tells his cellmate how he, every night, gets out of the prison and meets his wife on University Avenue; how they, holding hands, walk down the road and pick low-hanging mangoes; and how they make love beneath the stars. The cellmate knows the political prisoner cannot leave his cell. But he also can't help but notice the smell of mango coming from his bed and wafting all over the prison.

The City, 2014

No rain trees, only dreary condos
No haikus, only LED signs
No moon in no stream, only a bottle of local booze
Someone, please turn this bottle into a woman
Turn her legs into a bench so I can sit
Take her breath and change it into mountain mist
If these aren't possible, at least change my pen into a rifle
I want to take down the noisy motorbikes
Turning this night into hell

Lost Children (Thrown in the River), 2022

Miniaturist

A Buddha with no head
A supermarket without a past
A living room without shadows
Tiny mountains and waterfalls
When the light comes back on
Roaches scurry away

Maps on Their Palms

Men, women, and children line up in front of the immigration office waiting for their passports to be issued. A few hours have already passed and their bodies start to tremble. Their anguish quietly solidifies and becomes stones in their stomachs. Their anger hangs on their foreheads like poisonous fruits from a century-old garden. While the sun slowly moves overhead, their palms sweat and maps they have been carrying start to fade.

Tsunami

One minute it is vacant land and the next there are high-rise condos on it. Police find a suspicious package in one of the buildings and carry out a controlled explosion. An old man with white brows and small eyes mutters, "If you forget to turn off the tap, a tsunami will come. If you clap two times, a ghost will come haunt you. One spoon on your plate means a man will wait for you outside. Two spoons mean a woman will dream about you." There is a rainbow over the buildings, and children come out to see it. The old man continues, "If you drop a knife, a wild beast will show up at your doorstep. If you forget to turn off the tap, a tsunami will come . . ."

Human Hair Sleeps Too Long, 2018

Chrysanthemum

A flower is the alter ego of an ogre, a man's alter ego is a hermit crab. I walk past a garden of deranged flower beds. The antennae of human bugs point to a cluster of empty condos. The mist is gathering thick in the street and I try to touch its flesh to no avail. The chrysanthemums look as pale as water. I want to leave this place. It doesn't understand my eyes.

Temple-goers

Temple-goers go to the temple located at the foot of a mountain. An evil monk larger than the temple waits for them on their way and showers them with poisonous flowers. People who survive this attack go into the temple and make their wishes in front of the Buddha. They say it is worth it; they are so sure about the prospect of their wishes coming true.

The Soldier Dreams About Wild Horses, 2014

Reclining Buddha

The Buddha reclines under a banyan tree to nap and a boy sneaks into his body. There the boy sees villages moving as if they had a mind of their own; a rubber plantation and a butchered man lying in it, his cheeks transparent like tears; a woman cooking a meal for her children; and behind the Buddha's eyes: fire.

Strangler Fig

There is a strangler fig tree on the eastern border of a village. The villagers hang rice stalks, pieces of cloth, bars of soap, candles, and money from its branches. Every two or three days, monks come and gather the offerings. There is another strangler fig tree on the western end of the village which is covered with bloodied clothes, photos of missing children, belongings of fallen soldiers, hair of cancer patients, and dead butterflies. No one wants to see that tree. Many pretend it doesn't exist.

Rain Tree

"The rain tree got its name on account of it being rain-fed," said a rational man. A poet said, "It is called the rain tree because its leaves fall like rain." A cloud said, "It makes rain and that's how it got its name."

There was a time when farmers with debts hung themselves from rain trees. Trees bearing not raindrops but dead men.

Lost Children (The Rape), 2022

Irrawaddy Delta, 2016

A grain of rice cannot feed a hundred mouths
A solitary tree cannot house a thousand birds

The government doesn't speak for us
And we don't speak for the slain deer

We welcome a dawn
And drown it in the backwater

Flowers Downstream

When the farmer gets back to his farm, he sees the pigs lying dead all over the pen. A virus has got them. He sits on a carcass and grumbles something about the virus. A boat tied to a pole at the village pier dreams about distant harbors. Every day the village administrator receives complaint letters about a man-beast that runs about the village during the quiet hours of the night. No one knows where he comes from or where he hides. Meanwhile the population of the village has increased but there are not enough jobs. Somewhere upstream, a girl is raped and knifed to death. Her blood makes the water red and the flowers downstream turn blue.

Death in Summer

Flies lifting a carcass
Dry gourds dangling
Like an old woman's breasts
Mirages move quietly

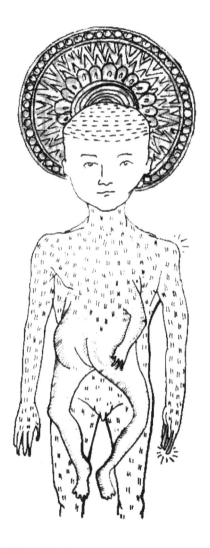

Lord, We Fished All Night And Caught Nothing, 2012

King Mindon's Soldier Poets

King Mindon birthed little creatures shaped like tadpoles. He fed them horse meat to make them grow. And they did, real fast. The king called them "soldier poets" on account of them chanting improvised verse when they were not fighting in wars.

King Mindon had an enemy. His younger brother also birthed little creatures he liked to call "oversexed poets" because they had sex all the time and looked like penises with human legs. They also liked to chant their silly poems.

Every fortnight, the two royal men staged a fight where the soldier poets and the oversexed ones fought each other to the death.

King Mindon and His Women

King Mindon was a jerk. When his women were building a palace for him using their hair, he was watching horse races. He had ordered his women to eat aloe vera and nothing else. "Eat that shit. It will help regrow your hair quickly," he told them. He also told his gardener to grow the same plant on every piece of vacant land surrounding the palace. People called him the Emerald King because when they thought about him, they only thought about the emerald-green aloe vera and not the ugliness hidden in it.

Lost Children 4, 2022

Black Bird

King Mindon liked to fuck, especially hookers. "I can do whatever I want to them," said the king with a broad grin. He would wear the coat adorned with little silver bells and go to the whorehouses. The hookers shook with terror upon hearing the sound of the silver bells. After having his way with the women, the king turned himself into a big black bird and pecked their stomachs open. The next day, his soldiers would go and clean up the mess.

King Mindon's Favorite Shoes

Every morning, after getting up from bed, King Mindon put on his favorite shoes and took a walk in the garden. The shoes were made from the skin of soldiers who died while serving in his army. The king thought making shoes from their skin was an act of genuine tribute, and he kept more than a hundred pairs.

Lost Children 2, 2022

Earthquakes

A town prone to earthquakes and therefore under a perpetual reconstruction. After a few generations, the townspeople start to get tired of it all. They say, "We can't just let these damn earthquakes come and bully us." So they decide to confront the earthquakes in their own way. After another one hits the town, they come out on the streets carrying various musical instruments and play them very loudly. Those who don't possess any musical instruments bang their pots and pans and water tanks with sticks. It's not only fun, but it also gives their action some sort of meaning. They do it again after another earthquake and again. They call the earthquakes "small deaths" and their response "rebirth."

What Monsoon Doesn't Know, 2014

Pink Mist

Everyone hates traffic jams and they keep getting worse. Cars on the bridge have not moved for more than an hour. Then someone who's had enough gets out of his car and everybody gets out of their car. Someone starts to levitate and everyone starts to levitate, their bodies slowly disintegrating into pink mist. The whole sky is a dark shade of pink, and under it, a completely silent bridge.

University of Noise

They go to the University of Noise to study the impact of ever-growing noises in the society. Some behavioral changes in animals and plants such as crickets no longer mating, a large number of dogs losing their desire to eat, and frangipani trees becoming barren are a few examples of the impact. Fascinated by new findings, the students are always discussing and debating, creating a lot of noise in their classroom and in their heads. This leads to behavioral changes in themselves. They care about each other less than before, they start to lose sleep at night, and many couples break up around the same time. These students are often found sitting near a river or a lake, gazing at the water and suffering from a type of asphyxiation at the same time. When they visit their doctors, the doctors diagnose them with common diseases like asthma and depression. No one sees the link between the noise the students make and their behavioral changes. So the students keep studying the impact of noises in animals and plants, and continue to make their own noise in the classroom.

The Elephant Revelation, 2012

Family of Four, 1990

Mother sits on the kitchen floor
Picking out weevils from a bowl of rice

Father counts the ghosts
Walking past the house and down the street

Daughter counts the roses
That make the whole garden ruby red

And what's the son doing?
He is punching the earth
Because someone broke his toy gun

The Carriage

The home I was born in. First I thought it was a home. Then I grew up and realized it was in fact a carriage drawn by a malevolent creature, probably centuries old. My family and I have been taken to places, and we are never allowed to get off. We can't see the face of the creature. Don't know what it will do to us at the end of the journey. We don't talk much about it but I know everyone is scared to death.

Father Turned Us Into Plants, 2014

Mountains

Mountains are the conscious mind of the earth curved outward.
There are gardens of shadows and songs between the mountains
and the water. These gardens are my memories curved inward.
Palm trees slowly move toward the theater of the sun. At a
certain point, a few of them may stop and never move again. Old
strangler fig trees, for instance. The boy of my childhood sleeps in
midair above the water and quietly burns away in the sun while I
look on.

Backpacks

When the boy of my childhood visited me again, I was lying in
bed, but not sleeping. He said it wasn't a dream and then put
me in a backpack. He took me to a myriad of cities, harbors, and
airports, ending the journey in a locked room full of backpacks
piling up on the floor. He said that I was in all of those bags and
that the bags were me. He added, "You are a burden to me as I
am to you." Then he put the bag I was in among other bags.

My Duty is to Protect Him #2, 2012

Accident

Flies take photos of the dead man with their eyes. The dead man thinks about his wife and the coconut rice she cooked for him that morning. He thinks about the longest drought he experienced in his life. He survived it and survived the civil war too. But now it has only needed a reckless driver and there he is, lying in a pool of blood.

One can see the clouds moving effortlessly in the glass windows of the shops. People continue to go about doing their things.

Art Exhibition

The city plans a big art exhibition dedicated to fire, its indestructible beauty and power. It is to take place at the city's art museum and all the budget for art is going to be spent on it. The posters say a hundred burning mattresses will be the centerpiece of the exhibition. At night while the city is asleep, people with burn marks come out quietly and spray-paint images of fire extinguishers all over the city to show their disapproval. The elevators go up and down cursing at fire.

Lost Children 1, 2022

Annual Checkups

The doctor looks at the charts and says everything, from her blood circulation to her nervous system, is right as rain. All the organs, including the uterus, the bladder, the heart, are healthy as hippos. In addition, she says her body produces something that defends her from hepatitis B, meaning she doesn't need to be vaccinated against that disease. The doctor says the same things every year, gives her the same results. A girlfriend of hers also gets perfect results every year. "Maybe she is just trying to keep every customer happy," she says to herself.

Every night, the general who rules the country sits in front of a camera and says all is well and everyone has every reason to be happy. "The general, like my doctor, is trying to keep everyone happy. But at least one should be aware of faked medical results," she reminds herself.

A Beautiful Morning

A man gets up from bed and opens the window. He sees a blue
sky and a new day welcoming him. A bird rests on the windowsill
and sings a pretty song. And he finds a fat wad of money on
his way to work. His neighbor also gets up in the morning
and makes some coffee. He is about to sit and enjoy his coffee
when he hears a knock on the door. He opens it and sees a boy
standing, his small face red with anger. The boy kicks the man
in the legs and says, "I know you have bad thoughts. Bad, bad
thoughts." After that, the boy leaves. If something has to happen,
it will happen. And that something can happen to anyone.

Festival of New Crops, 2018

Balance

He has nine duplicates of himself. It isn't like his existence has halted and his duplicates continue living his life at the point where he left off. It's more like he himself is a duplicate. A copy of the other copies. What he and the other duplicates do is try to create balance in the world. They try to cancel out each other's actions. When one duplicate commits murder, another saves a life by donating his blood at a blood bank. When one duplicate goes somewhere in a car, another deflates cars parked in the street. His knife goes deep into the rubber. He and the other duplicates believe this chaotic world could benefit from a little bit of balance and they all mean to create that balance.

Family Portrait

Our father died today. We have decided to take a family photo as a manner of saying goodbye to him. We have also planned a family dinner. After cooking, our mother comes into the living room and takes a pill. That's for her fatty liver, or maybe for her tired heart. Cicadas come into the house as the rain starts to fall. Then my sister walks in wearing a dress of fragile things. Her little boy touches the cicadas with his fingertips, and giggles like a leaking thatched roof. It's monsoon, which the cicadas hate. My brother-in-law is still at work. When the photographer arrives mumbling something about the rain, we are about to have dinner. My sister calls out to my dead father, and he comes out of his room. He is still drugged up but he sees us. Sees our black dog following him. He sits among us for the photo that we take without my brother-in-law who may be working overtime. After the photoshoot, my father gets up and walks back to his room. My sister says to him, "Dad, can I keep your pen as a keepsake, the one with the floral engravings?" Father nods his head and goes into his room.

A Book of Dreams

I got three books from my father—two before his death, and one after. I got the first one when I was ten. It was about stars with beautiful names that I tried to memorize by saying them aloud over and over. The second book came when I turned eighteen. A book of poems by Rabindranath Tagore. I got the last one from him in a dream after he died. It was a book of dreams he dreamt. I've had dreams borrowed from it.

I Am a House

My feet touching the earth are the roof. When I sit down at
the dinner table, which is in flames, my hand holding the spoon
catches on fire. I am not a garden but birds alight on me. They
are not aware that summer has arrived. They are not aware that
summer has arrived in my body. It's impossible to outlast seasons,
or time, a tongue that eats up houses and everything that lives in
them.

The Heir I, 2018

I Am an Empty Field

after Francis Ponge's "Rain"

I wake up with a sense of belief every morning. Compared to other forms of earth, my soil is richer. When it rains, water falls on my skin and goes into my body. By the time it reaches my lungs, it is already warm.

If the birds that fly carrying seedlings had seen me even once, I could have received most of the seedlings for myself. Like those birds, I have seen lightning strike innocent children. They were lucky the lightning was just a shaft of vapor every time. Unlike the seedling carriers, the birds that carry the spawn of witches always find me. I wish I had rabies so they might leave me alone. Now that they always see me, I decide to hide in the narrowest ravine. I roll myself like a carpet and tumble down. I decide to call the raindrops clinging to my body "sweat," and I paint my low morale brown. That's totally necessary, I tell myself.

I am some miles off the nearest conversation of men, but I know the bad things they would be saying about me. I am not always full of hope, but I hold on to some kind of belief. Although the nearest village is a great distance away, I like to offer a piece of myself to it as a gift. A piece of me that could become one with the village land. But for now, I hide myself in a ravine and become a ravine. It's temporary, but having to deal with the animals that inhabit me sucks. When I become a large field once again, I don't want to be static, but a moving organism. I know to become that, I need to be able to sit quietly and absorb light, then try to grow some legs, so I may be able to walk, not roll down the hills. I've seen dry branches of trees turn into insects, and stones flower buds. That means I could also become what I want to. There may also be opposite outcomes like being sucked into quicksand or being cut into small pieces. Another bad outcome is rainwater may shrink me or wash me away. Nonetheless I wake up with a positive belief every morning, and that belief is an infinite resource.

Acknowledgements

I am very grateful to Zeyar Lynn, Moe Way, Phyu Mon, Mrat Lunn Htwann, Moe Satt, Min Khet Ye, Aung Pyi Sone, Moe Thet Han, Nathan Hoks, James Byrne, Colin Cheney, Kaitlin Rees, and James Shea for giving me inspiration, showing me doors to open, and being good friends throughout the years. I would also like to thank Greg Bem. He reads my drafts, shares his thoughts with much honesty, and always lends an ear to whatever I want to say. I owe so much to the folks at Chin Music Press, especially Bruce Rutledge, Justine Chan, and Adriana Campoy, for their steadfast support and bringing this book to life.

Maung Day is a Burmese poet, artist, and translator.
He lives and works in Yangon, Burma/Myanmar.

Also by Maung Day

Poetry (in Burmese)

Pleasure Sea
Surplus Biology
Alluvial Plain of Ogres
Poems
Films: Poems
The Green Book
Spooky Action at a Distance
Our Predicaments
Gasoline (chapbook in English)

Fiction (in Burmese)

The Child Guest & Other Stories

Selected Translations (from English to Burmese)

Paranoia Is Poetry: Translations of Works by 15 International Poets
with Commentaries
Selected Poems of Russell Edson
Selected Poems of Carlos Drummond de Andrade
Selected Poems of Maram al-Masri
Selected Haiku of Kobayashi Issa
Selected Poems of Chika Sagawa
Kitchen by Banana Yoshimoto
Haroun and the Sea of Stories by Salman Rushdie

Printed in the USA
CPSIA information can be obtained
at www.ICGtesting.com
JSHW051500291023
51054JS00002B/2